Cats and
Bats and Things
with Wings

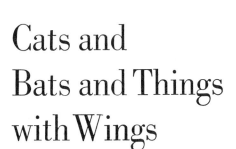

Cats and
Bats and Things
with Wings

Poems by
Conrad Aiken

Drawings by
Milton Glaser

Atheneum

New York

Text copyright © 1965
by Conrad Aiken
Illustrations copyright © 1965
by Milton Glaser
All rights reserved
Library of Congress
catalog card number: 65-21724
Published simultaneously in Canada
by McClelland & Stewart Ltd.
Manufactured in
the United States of America
Printed by
Reehl Litho, Inc., New York
Bound by H. Wolff, New York
First Printing July 1965
Second Printing January 1966
Third Printing August 1966
Fourth Printing February 1967
Fifth Printing June 1968
Sixth Printing October 1969
Seventh Printing August 1971
Eighth Printing January 1973
Ninth Printing September 1975

The artist wishes to express
his thanks to Motif Magazine,
London, in which some of
the illustrations originally appeared.

This book
for
Madge Bird Lloyd
a friend
to
all children
of
all ages

For Estelle

CONTENTS

The Crocodile.

O crocodile
that ancient smile
old as the Congo
or the Nile
and full of wile
and full of guile
o crocodile
dear crocodile
ARE you mayhap
a tourist trap
ready to snap
at you
or me
and
    TAKE
        US
           KINDLY
               IN
                 TO
                   TEA?
Is there a tooth behind that smile
are we
to be
the tea?
Yet handsome he
and what a tail
and he can swing it
like a flail
hoping
of course
to knock us flat:
and, if he does,
that's THAT.
O you're a scalawag
scale-awag scalawag
tail-awag scalawag
that's what you are
that's what!

The Cat.

Who would not love
a cat
like
that?
Fluffy and fat
and kind is he
and O as gentle as can be
and when I ask him says to me
My name is *Ollie*.
You might prefer
a kinky cur
perhaps a collie
or a dolly
or even a firetruck
or a trolley
but as for me
I'd rather be
right here beside the fire for tea
with *Ollie* on my knee.
His eyes are always changing, too:
sometimes they're green
and sometimes blue:
and now and then I've seen
deep in his secret dark of night
his two eyes blazing bright
as if *two moons* were shining there
at top of stair.
Mysterious!
Whiskerious!
Imperious!
That
is
cat.

The Octopus.

The many-handed octopus
does not INTEND to frighten us:
his family name is octopod
and certainly he is odd.
A kind of spider of the sea
is he.
Lovely to watch him waver round
under the sea without a sound
and how he folds
     and then unfolds
        shapes
          and then reshapes
            drapes
              and then undrapes
each slithery arm and hand
and
still always can
come back to where he first began.
O what a juggler he could be:
the greatest juggler of the sea:
eight balls at once he'd keep with ease
above his head beneath the seas
passing from one to other
without the slightest bother.
But if WE frighten HIM
then suddenly all goes dim
behind a cloud of ink
he seems to shrink
and off unseen he'll swiftly swim
upon a pearly oyster bed
to lay his troubled head.

The Grasshopper.

Grasshopper
grasshopper
all day long
we hear your scraping
summer song
      like
          rusty
              fiddles
                  in
          the
        grass
as through
        the meadow
            path
              we pass
such funny legs
such funny feet
and how we wonder
what you eat
maybe a single blink of dew
sipped from a clover leaf would do
then high in air
      once more you spring
          to fall in grass again
              and sing.

The Rhinoceros.

Beware lest you should get a toss
from grumpy old Rhinoceros
bad-tempered he
so cautiously
we'd better
keep   our   distance—
see?
Is he the fabled unicorn?
For he too wore a single horn
but he we learn
was gentle born
and when he spied
a maid forlorn
lost in the darkest forest
he
would lay his head
upon her knee
then guide her
safely
home
to
tea.
Not so old grump Rhinoceros
who'd rather give us all a *toss*.

The Owl.

To whit
to whoo
he stares
right through
whatever
he looks at
maybe
YOU
and so
whatever
else
you do
don't
    ever
       ever
          be
            a
              mouse
           or
          if
       you
are
    STAY
       IN
          YOUR
             HOUSE
old owl
can you be really
wise
and do those great big
sunflower eyes
see THINGS
that WE
can never see
perched on the tiptop of your tree

or by jiminy
on a chimney
or whooshing by
on velvet wings?
Let's hie to bed
and leave him be.

The Seal.

How must it feel
to be
a
seal
and swish among the
ducks
and teal
and swim
a cool
Virginia Reel
right underneath
somebody's
keel?
Then
much
to
somebody's surprise
pop up your head
right out of sea
and blink your big blue baby eyes
and flap your fins
with glee?
And o what bliss
on summer days
what bliss it is
to lie and laze
on a warm mudflat
in the sun
and *sunbathe*
just
like
anyone.
I think the seal
has
all
the
fun.

The Goats.

One two three four
five six seven
all good goats
will go to heaven
what kind of heaven
will it be?
A hill, and on the hill
a tree
where robin redbreast
pipes his glee.
There they will go
in Sunday coats
the Billy goats
and Nanny goats
to wet their beards
in dripping grass
and crunch and munch
tin cans and glass
or in a lovely trashpile look
to see if they can find
a *book*—
just like this one
made of paper
and chew the leaves
and give a caper:
Billy and Nanny
kids and all
until at milking time
they call
meh-eh-eh-eh,
leap on a wall
then peacefully
stroll home
to stall.

The Mandrill.

In the Mandrill
unrefined
Beauty and Beast
are well combined.
How would *you* like
to have that face
to look at in your looking-glass?
And all the other
jungle creatures
what must *they* think
of those strange features?
And that odd name
the Mandrill—can
it be he hopes
to BE a *man?*
But *that* face
won't
wash
off
with
soap:
I fear poor Mandrill
has
no
hope.

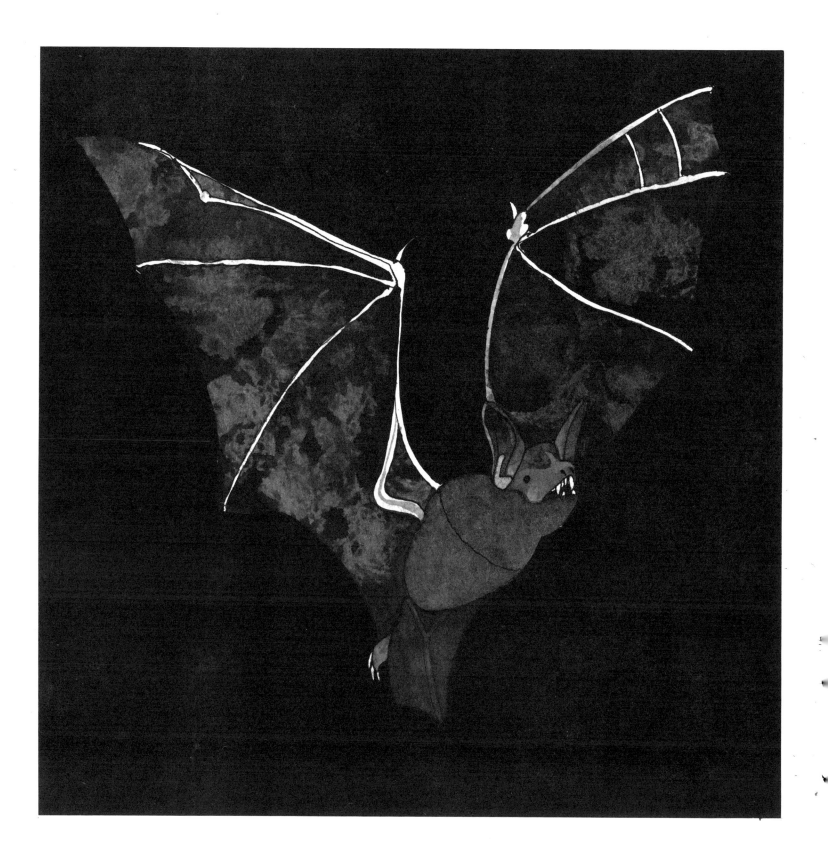

The Bat.

What's that—?
A bat!
And what's a bat?
    And IF a bat
        then
            what's
                he
                  at?
Perhaps he wants a nice fat gnat.
On noiseless wings
see how he swoops
in circles
dives
and loop-the-loops.
The darkness never frightens HIM
he likes it BEST
when it is dim:
and he's so skilful
        he
           can
              skim
right past
        a
           chimney
              or
              a
                wall
and never touch
           the
              thing
                at
              all.

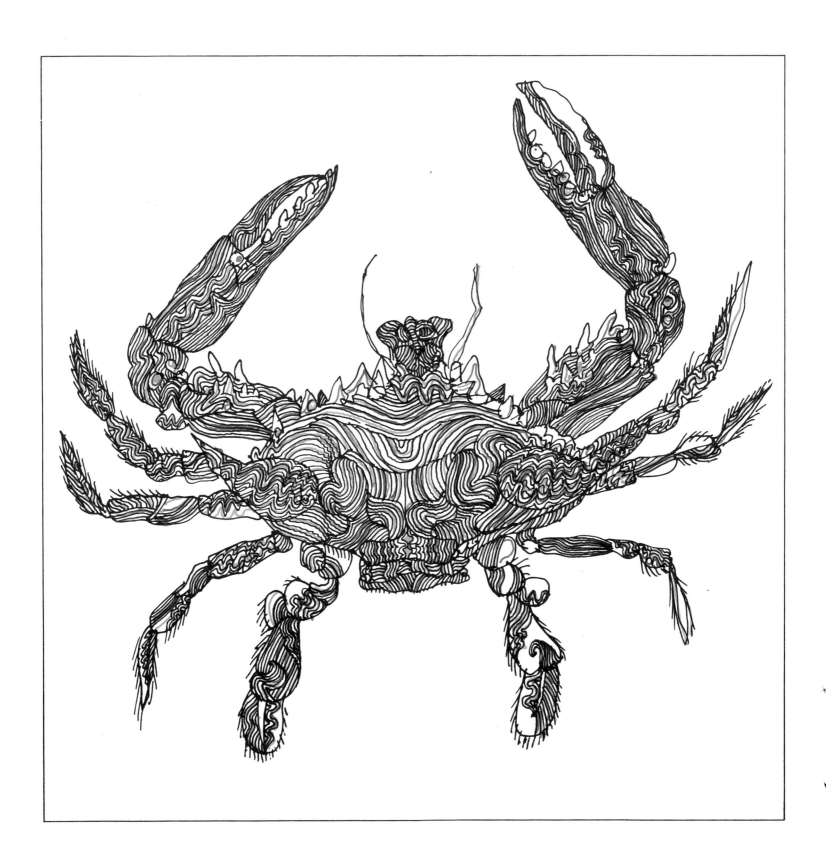

The Crab.

Don't ever grab
old crusty crab
because
with all those claws
he'll maybe grab you first
and you'll come off the worst!
I knew a small boy long ago
o long and long and long ago
whose mother said she did not know
just where the crab's *eyes* were: and so
he pointed with his finger, and
that crab politely took his hand
as if to say let's take a walk
and have a talk
upon this lovely seaside wharf:
and had to be *flung off:*
but on his finger left a dent
that lasted *days* before it went.
He doesn't sing he isn't mean
in fact he keeps the water clean
by eating up the scraps galore
that litter up the ocean's floor:
and if at times he *can* be vicious
remember he is *so* nutritious
and O in soups delicious!
(Perhaps it's mean
to mention a tureen.)
Old crusty crab, all claws no head,
he scuttles on the ocean bed
but never said
or so I've heard
a single crusty
or crustacean
word.

The Cassowary.

Behold the scraggly cassowary
who is so very very *very*
hairy—and big—and see
his toes are three.
And why three?
Don't ask *me*.
And such legs
and such eggs
and that eye
that asks you *why?*
Why indeed have such a breed
and did we really *need?*
But then that very very
wary ancient cassowary
can say to us *you too—*
why *you?*
A question we had better beg
or eat the cassowary's egg.

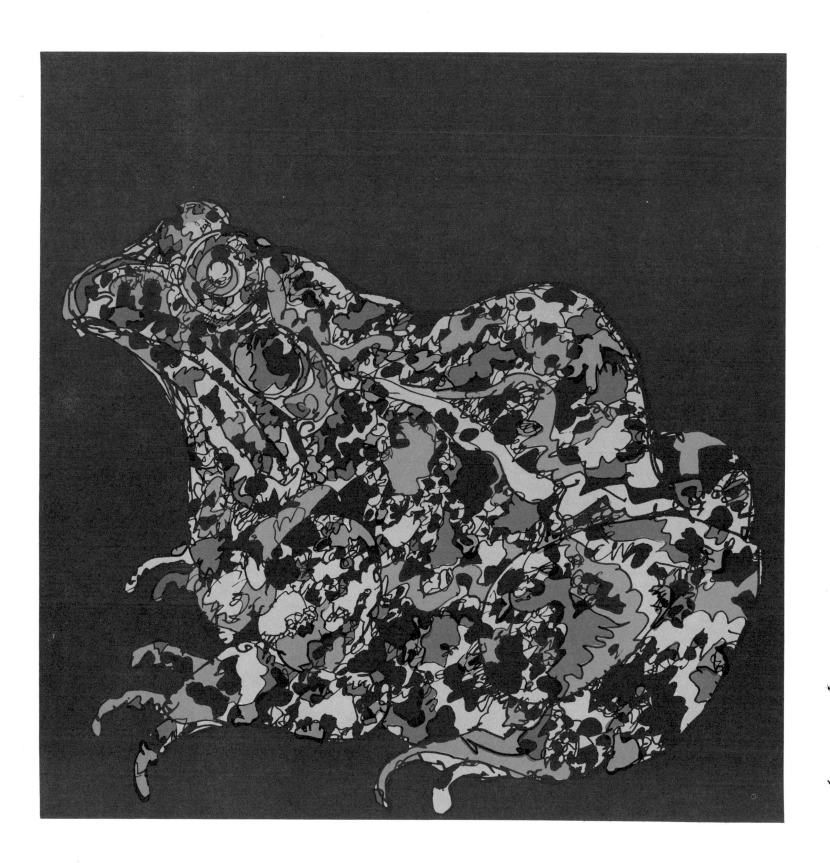

The Frog.

How nice to be
       a
       speckled
       frog
with all those
       colors
       in
       a
       bog
AND SIT THERE ALL DAY LONG AND SOG
how nice at noon
to keep so cool
just squatting in your private pool
or when enough of THAT you've had
       to sun
       on
    your own lily pad.
But best of all at rise of moon
with you
and all your friends
in tune
as *jug-o'-rum*
and *jing-a-ring*
and trilling *peep-peep-peep*
you sing
till
   listening
       we
          fall
            asleep
               slowly
          listening
    fall
asleep.

The Lion.

The lion is a lordly thing
and rightly of the beasts called **King**
o yes indeed the King of Beasts
just so it's not on *us* he feasts
those golden eyes
how piercing wise
those powerful paws
those cutting claws
and o those mighty jaws
these are enough and more
even without a roar
to give us pause.
Those claws can rip a plank right through
those jaws can chew
a bone in two
he is a fearful sight
by day or night
of might.
But let's remember too
he has a beauty unsurpassed
see by the moon his shadow cast
upon a desert dune
or silhouetted on the moon
those sinewy shoulders and that mane
while thrice he roars
and roars again
proclaiming far and near
to norths to souths to wests to easts
Look and fear
your King is here
I am the King of Beasts!

The Fallow Deer.

The fallow deer
how lovely he
with horns
just like
a Christmas Tree
that is
if you put
spangles on
and tinsel on
and bangles on
and he's as gentle
as can be
so meek
so mild
that any child
can feed him with her hand
and stand
and stare
he doesn't
care.
You ask me
why they call him
fallow
it is because
he's
kind of yallow
when he is young
he has a dapple
and
o
my
how
he
loves
an
apple.

The Elephant.

The elephant grows very old
he lives to years untold
and as you see he's *mani*fold:
with folds and folds of rubbery skin
some tucked out and some tucked in
his eye
is shy
and he is humorous and sly.
And o my how he loves a tub
and someone with a brush to scrub
those folds and kinks
and clean
his toes and all that's in between
while with his trunk he drinks
and sprays his back and *winks*.
Then when the bath is done
he thinks it's fun
to dunk
his trunk
and squirt his back all over
with dust and straws and clover.
Old elephant is clever:
he never
forgets:
but lets
something he sees stay in his mind
while years and years unwind:
if someone is unkind
he'll find
a way to punish the unkind one.
But to the *kind* one
he'll go down on his knees
as if to say
I don't forget that day
long ago and far away
when you were good to me:
my memory never ends:
let us be friends.